A PHOTO-FACT BOOK

TEXT AND PHOTOGRAPHS
BY
GEORGE HALL

Copyright ©1989 by Kidsbooks, Inc.
7004 N. California Ave.
Chicago, Illinois 60645

ISBN 0-942025-95-4

Manufactured in the
United States of America

➤ INTRODUCTION ➤

The fighter jets get all the glory, but many different aircraft types are required to bring the war to the enemy. Although fighter pilots hate to admit it, their main job is to protect the attack planes as they go about the difficult and dangerous job of putting their weapons on target.

The attack jets aren't as fast, sleek, or maneuverable as the fighters, but they pack a tremendous wallop. Carrier-based bombers like the A-6E Intruder can carry as big a bomb load as the largest World War II strategic bombers, and their amazing electronic systems allow them to place the weapons on the target with computer-controlled accuracy in even the worst weather and darkness. The FB-111 and the four-engine B-1 bombers are capable of supersonic dashes to targets at great distances from the United States.

We'll also be looking at some other specialized aerial attackers, including the AH-64 Apache, a hi-tech Army helicopter that possess the speed and carrying capacity of earlier-generation attack airplanes. The amazing AV-8B Harrier is the free world's only VSTOL (Vertical or Short Takeoff and Landing) jet, able to fly at near-supersonic speeds and hover motionless before landing vertically like a helicopter. Then there's the awesome A-10 Thunderbolt, a rough-looking Air Force attack jet designed to support ground troops by shooting enemy armored vehicles.

Rounding out our survey will be the Panavia Tornado, a modern twin-jet fighter-bomber-interceptor flown by our European allies in NATO, the North Atlantic Treaty Organization. The little F-5 Tiger fighter-bomber is an American-made jet that is flown by almost 50 other friendly air forces around the world. And we'll also climb into the back seat of the sleek T-38 Talon, the principal advanced training jet for future Air Force fighter and attack pilots.

F-5 Aggressors in various enemy camouflage paint schemes.

F-5 TIGER II

The handsome little F-5, a twin-jet supersonic fighter-bomber, is built in America. It has been designed only as an export fighter, to be used by friendly air forces around the world that need a hot jet that's simple to operate and maintain. The US Air Force and Navy have a few Tigers, too. They use them as "Aggressors," flying them against our fighter and attack pilots in simulation of enemy tactics. These Aggressor jets are usually painted in a variety of strange camouflage patterns, such as those commonly used in Communist or Third World countries. And like most Soviet planes, they carry large outlined nose numbers painted beneath the canopies.

Remember those ominous black MiG-28s that menaced Maverick and Iceman in TOP GUN? In reality they were F-5s of the Navy Fighter Weapons School, painted in wash-off black paint and flown by Top Gun instructors. The F-5 really isn't as strong as a modern military jet, but in skilled hands its small size and great maneuverability can turn it into a very nasty dogfight opponent.

F-5E Tiger II
Nickname: F-5

MISSION: Tactical fighter
POWER PLANT: Two General Electric J85-GE-21 turbojet engines
THRUST: 5,000 pounds each engine with afterburner
SPEED: Mach 1.6 (1,280 mph) at 36,000 feet
CEILING: 51,800 feet
ARMAMENT: Two AIM-9 Sidewinder missiles; variety of air-to-surface ordnance on five pylons; two M-39 20mm cannons with 560 rounds of ammunition
MAXIMUM WEIGHT AT TAKEOFF: 26,000 pounds
CREW: Pilot

The Navy's TOP GUN school uses the F-5 as a "bad guy" simulator.

FB-111

The huge FB-111 is a longer-range strategic version of the F-111 fighter-bomber. The "FB" stands for fighter-bomber, but this hulking airplane is far more bomber than fighter, since it can weigh over 100,000 pounds on takeoff! The 111 series has never had a real name, but it's universally known as the "Aardvark" because of its long, droopy, radar-filled snout.

The 'Vark is a twin-engine bird, carrying two of the same TF-30 turbofans that power the F-14 Tomcat. And like the F-14 it has "variable-geometry" wings that swing into different positions for fast or slow flight. It's a dual crew plane, with the pilot sitting on the left and the navigator-bombardier on his right. The right-seater has no flight controls; he worries about the weapons systems while the pilot does all the flying.

Despite its immense size and weight, the 'Vark is very, very fast, especially "on the deck," or only a few feet above the ground. It can easily exceed the speed of sound—about 725 mph at sea level—in low-level flight. That's a feat that very few military jets can manage. It is also fitted with an amazing terrain-avoidance radar system that actually flies the jet among the hills and valleys with only a few yards of altitude to spare!

FB-111
Nickname: Aardvark

MISSION: Medium-range strategic bomber
POWER PLANT: Two Pratt & Whitney TF30-P-7 turbofan engines with variable afterburners
THRUST: 20,350 pounds each engine
SPEED: Mach 2.5 (2,000 mph) at 36,000 feet
CEILING: Above 60,000 feet
ARMAMENT: Four AGM-69A SRAM air-to-surface missiles on external pylons and two in weapons bay, or six nuclear bombs, or combinations of these weapons; provision for up to 31,500 pounds of conventional bombs
MAXIMUM WEIGHT AT TAKEOFF: Approximately 100,000 pounds
CREW: Two—Pilot and navigator/bombardier

The FB-111 is a long-range version of the F-111 fighter-bomber.

AV-8B HARRIER II

The Harrier has a unique talent—it's a VSTOL jet, meaning it can vector its jet thrust nozzles to takeoff and land vertically. This allows the Harrier to be operated from open clearings, roads, or ship decks that are scarcely larger than the jet itself. After lifting off like a hummingbird, the Harrier can rotate its jet nozzles aft and blast to near-supersonic speeds (650 mph-plus) in just a few seconds.

The AV-8 Harrier is a British creation and is flown by British Air Force and Naval units. The first batch of Harriers used by the U.S. Marine Corps were made in England. The new B-model, pictured, is a much-improved version of the original, with a more powerful engine, better flight stability, and sophisticated weapons-delivery systems. Its 21,500 pounds of thrust is a tremendous amount of power for a single engine. That kind of raw thrust is necessary to pick up a fully-loaded jet vertically into the air.

British and Marine pilots have learned that by turning the thrust nozzles in flight, they can "VIF" (that stands for "vector in flight") the little jet into incredibly tight turns. Although the Harrier was designed as a ground attack jet rather than a fighter, it has proven to be a formidable dogfighter because of its unique talents.

AV-8B Harrier II
Nickname: None

MISSION: Attack jet
POWER PLANT: One Rolls Royce Pegasus fanjet engine
THRUST: 21,500 pounds with vectored-thrust exhaust nozzles
SPEED: High subsonic (650 mph)
CEILING: 51,000 feet
ARMAMENT: 25mm cannon; variety of bombs, rockets, and air-to-air missiles
MAXIMUM WEIGHT AT TAKEOFF: 24,600 pounds
CREW: Pilot

An AV-8B Harrier hovers atop 21,500 pounds of jet thrust.

A-6E INTRUDER

The Intruder will never win any beauty contests; in fact with its bulbous nose and pointed tail cone, it almost looks as if it's flying in the wrong direction! But enemies long ago learned not to laugh at this formidable bomber and its capabilities. The A-6E is the Navy's heavy carrier-based bomber, designed to operate from pitching steel decks in even the worst weather conditions. It can be catapulted into the air with nine tons of weaponry hanging from its underwing stations—that's more ordnance than our big B-17 four-engine bombers were able to carry in World War II.

The Intruder, like the FB-111, carries a two-man crew seated side-by-side. The bombardier in the right seat flies into battle with his head down, eyeing his weapons computers, radar screen, navigation instruments, and FLIR (forward-looking infrared) sensors that allow him to see targets on the ground at night. And then, after the wrenching pull off of the target, it's back to the ship for the scariest part of the mission—landing the big Intruder down on the carrier's rolling steel deck.

A-6E Intruder
Nickname: Buff

MISSION: Destroy moving and fixed, sea and land targets, in all weather conditions, and during darkness
POWER PLANT: Two Pratt & Whitney J52-P8B turbojet engines
THRUST: 9,300 pounds each engine
SPEED: High subsonic (650 mph)
CEILING: 40,600 feet
ARMAMENT: 15,000 pounds of bombs, rockets, nuclear weapons, and air-to-surface missiles
MAXIMUM WEIGHT AT TAKEOFF: 58,600 pounds
CREW: Two—Pilot and navigator/bombardier

A-6E Intruders, the aircraft carrier's heavy-duty bomber.

AH-64 APACHE

The Army is used to relying on the Air Force for close-air support when it's locked in battle. But now the Army is fielding its own hi-tech attack craft, the fearsome AH-64 Apache.

The Apache is an attack weapons platform that can streak over the ground at almost 200 mph.

It can carry an awesome array of weaponry, including rockets, laser-guided Hellfire missiles for taking out tanks, and conventional bombs. In addition it has a chin-mounted 25mm machine gun that is connected to the copilot's helmet electronically—the gun will point instantly and automatically wherever he looks.

The Apache's two crewmen are both qualified pilots. The man in back does most of the flying, while the front-seater handles the shooting and the navigating. Pilots in Apache units rotate regularly between the two seats so that all are accomplished at both functions.

AH-64 Apache
Nickname: None

MISSION: Attack of armored tanks; troop support
POWER PLANT: Two General Electric T700-GE-701 turboshaft engines, 1,696 horsepower each engine
SPEED: 192 mph
CEILING: 21,000 feet
ARMAMENT: 30mm automatic cannon; 16 Hellfire or TOW (Tube-launched, Optically tracked, Wire-guided missiles); 76 FFAR (folding-fin aerial rockets)
MAXIMUM WEIGHT AT TAKEOFF: 21,000 pounds
CREW: Two—Pilot and copilot/gunner

An Army AH-64 Apache attack helicopter loaded with rockets and Hellfire anti-tank missiles.

# PANAVIA TORNADO

The Tornado was developed in the early 1970s by Great Britain, West Germany, and Italy.

The Tornado is very fast, very powerful, and very capable. It is produced in two different versions, a fighter-interceptor for aerial defense and a fighter-bomber for all-weather ground attack. It has two afterburning engines, swing wings, and a crew of two in tandem—pilot up front and radar intercept officer in the "pit," or back seat.

NATO Tornados routinely intercept Soviet reconnaissance flights over the North Sea and in the Atlantic Ocean northwest of Ireland. One intercept in September of 1988 was just a bit different—two Royal Air Force Tornados met a pair of Russian MiG-29 Fulcrums that were flying into English air space from a base in East Germany. But these hot Soviet jets were invited guests at the famous Farnborough Air Show near London. No one present will ever forget the excitement of their arrival—the two handsome green-and-gray Russian jets bracketed on either wing by a Tornado in full wing sweep; the jets streaking low over the crowd in a flawless four-plane formation.

Panavia Tornado
Nickname: None

MISSION: Fighter/bomber
POWER PLANT: Two turbo-union RB-199 turbofans with afterburners
THRUST: 16,000 pounds each engine
SPEED: Mach 2 (1,600 mph) at 40,000 feet
CEILING: Above 50,000 feet
ARMAMENT: 27mm Mauser cannon; variety of bombs, rockets, and air-to-air missiles
MAXIMUM WEIGHT AT TAKEOFF: 60,000 pounds
CREW: Two—Pilot and weapons systems officer

The Panavia Tornado is a twin-jet interceptor flown by several NATO air forces in Europe.

➤ B-1B BOMBER ➤

America's newest and most potent strategic bomber is the B-1B, now in full operation out of four Strategic Air Command bases in the US. The new jet has taken the load off the aging fleet of B-52 Stratofortress bombers, most of which are over 25 years old. A group of B-1Bs are kept on strategic alert 24 hours a day, ready to take off on a few minutes notice to attack with conventional or nuclear weapons.

The B-1B is a four-engine aircraft. Each engine is fitted with afterburners that can boost the total thrust to more than 120,000 pounds. A crew of four sits up front in ejection seats—pilot and copilot facing forward, two electronic wizards facing rear toward their control consoles. Almost thirty tons of electronic gadgets are aboard to foil enemy radars and jam anti-aircraft weapons.

Although the B-1B is bigger than most airliners, its pilots report that it handles just like a huge fighter. Unlike most big jets, the B-1B pilot holds a fighter-style control stick instead of a wheel. Variable-geometry swing wings, controlled by computer as the jet varies its speed, can move back into an extreme delta shape for ultra-high-speed dashes into the target area.

B-1B Bomber
Nickname: None

MISSION: Strategic heavy bomber
POWER PLANT: Four General Electric F101-GE-102 turbofan engines with afterburners
THRUST: Approximately 30,000 pounds each engine
SPEED: Low supersonic; high subsonic for low-altitude penetration
CEILING: Classified
ARMAMENT: Variety of air-to-surface ordnance, including conventional bombs, "smart" guided bombs, strategic nuclear weapons or air-launched Cruise missiles
MAXIMUM WEIGHT AT TAKEOFF: 477,000 pounds
CREW: Four—Pilot, copilot, offensive systems operator, defensive systems operator

America's new strategic bomber is the B-1B.

A-10 THUNDERBOLT II

The A-10 has one job and one job only—close air support of ground troops, especially troops that are having trouble with enemy tanks and mechanized armor. As befits its down and dirty role, the A-10 is another ugly airplane. It's supposed to be known as the "Thunderbolt II," after the P-47 attack bomber of World War II fame, but everyone calls it the "Warthog."

The 'Hog was literally designed and built around its principal weapon, the GAU-8 Avenger cannon. This enormous Gatling gun, that's as big as a small car, is the heart of the A-10. It spews out armor-piercing 30mm projectiles at the rate of 65 per second. These bullets can melt their way through the armor plate of just about any tank. The plane also carries a variety of bombs, rockets, and Maverick anti-tank missiles.

Although the A-10 is powered by two big jets, it seldom does much beyond 250 mph over the battlefield. That's great for accurate shooting at the enemy, but the slow-moving 'Hog is unfortunately very easy to hit. In expectation of the worst, the A-10 is heavily armored, and all of its hydraulic control systems have three backups in case of severe damage. And the pilot sits encased in a titanium steel "bathtub," completely surrounding him and his ejection seat.

A-10 Thunderbolt II
Nickname: 'Hog, Warthog

MISSION: Close air support of ground troops
POWER PLANT: Two General Electric TF34-GE-100 turbofan engines
THRUST: 8,900 pounds each
SPEED: 423 mph
CEILING: Can operate under 1,000 feet with one-mile visibility
ARMAMENT: One GAU-8A 30mm, seven-barrel Gatling gun; up to 16,000 pounds mixed ordnance, including 500-pound retarded bombs, 2,000-pound general purpose bombs, incendiary and Rockeye II cluster bombs, Maverick missiles, laser-guided/electro-optically guided bombs, infrared countermeasure flares, electronic countermeasure chaff, and jammer pods
MAXIMUM WEIGHT AT TAKEOFF: 46,038 pounds
CREW: Pilot

The ugly A-10 Thunderbolt has just one job—to shoot up enemy armor with its huge 30mm cannon.

T-38 TALON

For over 20 years, the beautiful T-38 Talon has been the Air Force pilot's introduction to the amazing world of supersonic flight. Every pilot, even those who wind up flying heavy bombers or transports, will do some advanced instruction in this hot, supersonic trainer. It is a much-loved jet, fondly remembered by just about every Air Force pilot who ever "strapped it on."

The T-38's two jet engines are not really all that powerful, but its long, stiletto-like fuselage and little stubby wings make it a very slick performer. The T-38 is not particularly hard to fly, but like any good trainer it demands great precision and concentration. Many of the more modern jets, with their computer controls and stupendous power, are actually easier to fly. The best thing that can be said of any training aircraft can definitely be said of the Talon—if you've got "good hands" in this baby, you'll be able to handle any jet in the Air Force inventory.

T-38 Talon
Nickname: None

MISSION: Advanced supersonic trainer
POWER PLANT: Two Pratt & Whitney J-85 turbojets with afterburners
THRUST: 8,000 pounds each engine
SPEED: Mach 1.2 (960 mph)
CEILING: 53,600 feet
ARMAMENT: None
MAXIMUM WEIGHT AT TAKEOFF: 12,093 pounds
CREW: Two—student in front, instructor in rear

The T-38 Talon is the advanced jet trainer for Air Force pilots.

A-7 CORSAIR II

This Corsair is named after its World War II ancestor, the F-4U "hose nose," made famous by Pappy Boyington's Black Sheep squadron. The Corsair II, like so many funny-looking airplanes, has to suffer under the weight of other less reverent nicknames, like "the shoebox" or the "SLUF"—for Short Little Ugly Fella.

But regardless of looks, the A-7 can do the job. It's the principal light-attack jet on our Navy carriers, although it is gradually being replaced in this slot by the newer and far more capable F/A-18 Hornet. The Air Force also flies the SLUF—Air National Guard wings in six states operate some two hundred of the jets, all painted in ground-attack green instead of Navy ghost gray.

The A-7 can sling the usual array of nastiness under its wings—anti-personnel rockets, iron bombs, napalm, "smart" ordnance guided by either laser or on-board television cameras. In addition, it carries an internally-mounted 20mm rotary cannon, and it can pack a pair of Sidewinder heat-seeking anti-aircraft missiles on rails beneath the canopy. Of course, the Corsair isn't much of a dogfighter—it's too underpowered, and it doesn't crank around the corner very well—but a good SLUF pilot can still manage a couple of moves to put himself in Sidewinder shooting position dead astern of his bad guy.

A-7 Corsair II
Nickname: SLUF (Short Little Ugly Fella)

MISSION: Light attack jet
POWER PLANT: One Allison TF41-1 engine
THRUST: 14,250 pounds
SPEED: 690 mph
CEILING: 36,700 feet
ARMAMENT: One M-61 Vulcan cannon; 15,000 pounds of bombs and rockets; Sidewinder missiles
MAXIMUM WEIGHT AT TAKEOFF: 42,000 pounds
CREW: Pilot

The A-7 Corsair is a carrier-based, light attack jet.

An A-7 fires a 5" ZUNI rocket at a ground target.

The Air Force is considering an interesting plan to take the A-7 fighting into the 1990s. Its manufacturer, Vought Aircraft, has proposed a thorough modernization which will "stretch" the fuselage, drop in a much hotter afterburning engine, fit a couple of state-of-the-art wings, and cram the cockpit full of the latest avionics and weapons systems. The little SLUF would be transformed into a supersonic hummer that could tussle with the best attack jets in the sky—at the fraction of the cost for developing an all-new plane.

The attack pilots, the mud movers, the dirt-throwers—call them what you will. They don't get a lot of the glory, but they know the truth: they're the guys doing the real damage to the enemy. Regardless of the type of plane they fly, it takes special kinds of pilots to succeed on an attack mission. Manfred von Richtofen, the infamous "Red Baron" of World War I, said it best 75 years ago:

> "The crate? The quality of the crate matters
> little. Success depends on the man who sits in it."